Claude
DEBUSSY

DANSES
Sacrée et profane
CD 113
(1904)

Study Score
Partitur

PETRUCCI LIBRARY PRESS

CONTENTS

ORCHESTRA

Harp solo

Violins I

Violins II

Violas

Violoncellos

Double Basses

Duration: ca. 9 minutes

First performance: November 6, 1904
Paris: Concerts Colonne
Madame Wurmser-Delcourt, harp solo
Orchestra de Concerts Colonne / Édouard Colonne

ISBN: 978-1-60874-173-1
This score is a slightly modified unabridged reprint of the score
issued in 1904 by Durand et Fils, Paris, plate D. & F. 6419.
The score has been scaled to fit the present format.

Printed in the USA
First Printing: April, 2015

Danses Sacrée et Profane
CD 113

I. Danse sacrée

Claude Debussy
(1904)

Petrucci Library Press

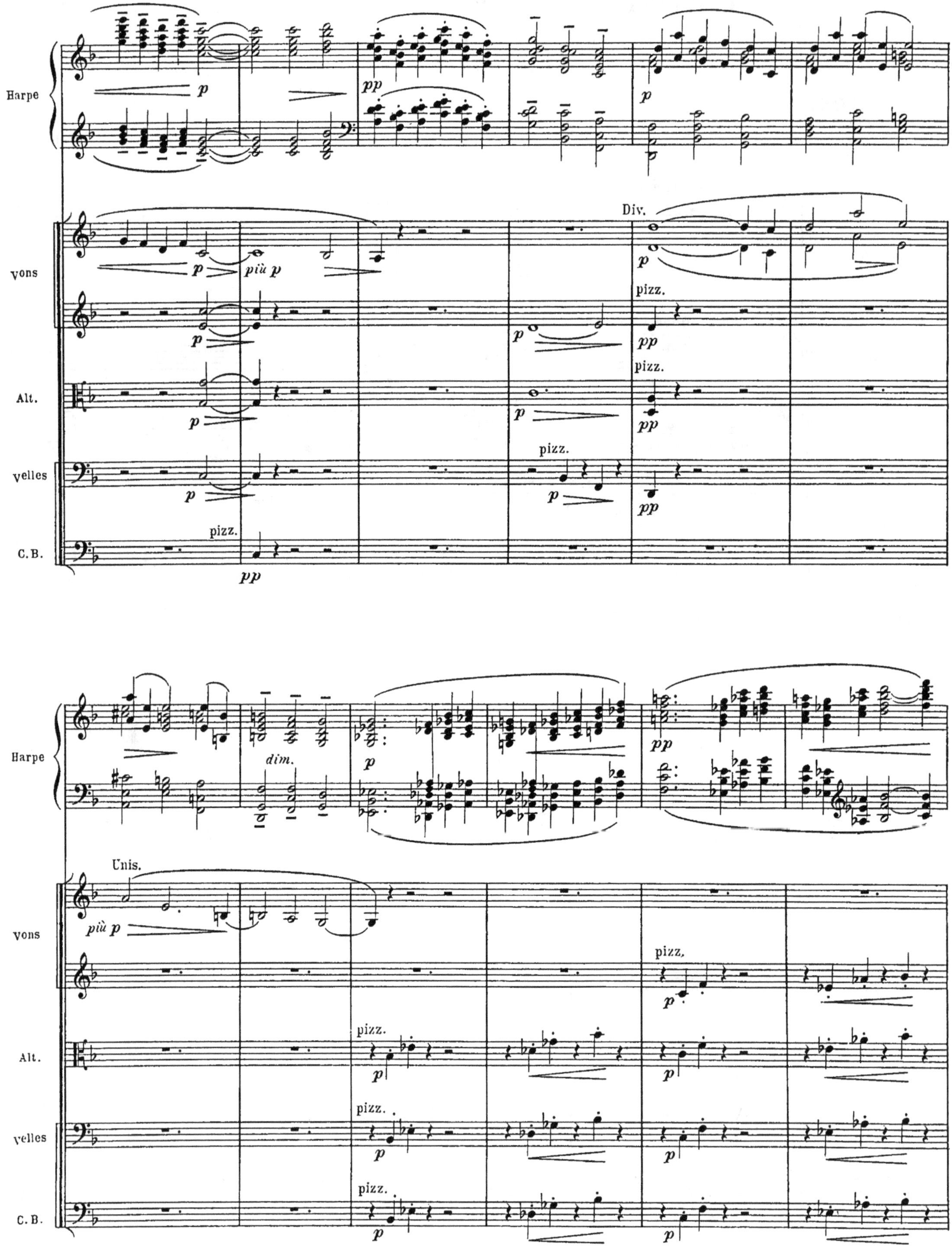
Harpe
vons
Alt.
velles
C.B.
p
pp
più p
pizz.
Div.
Unis.
dim.

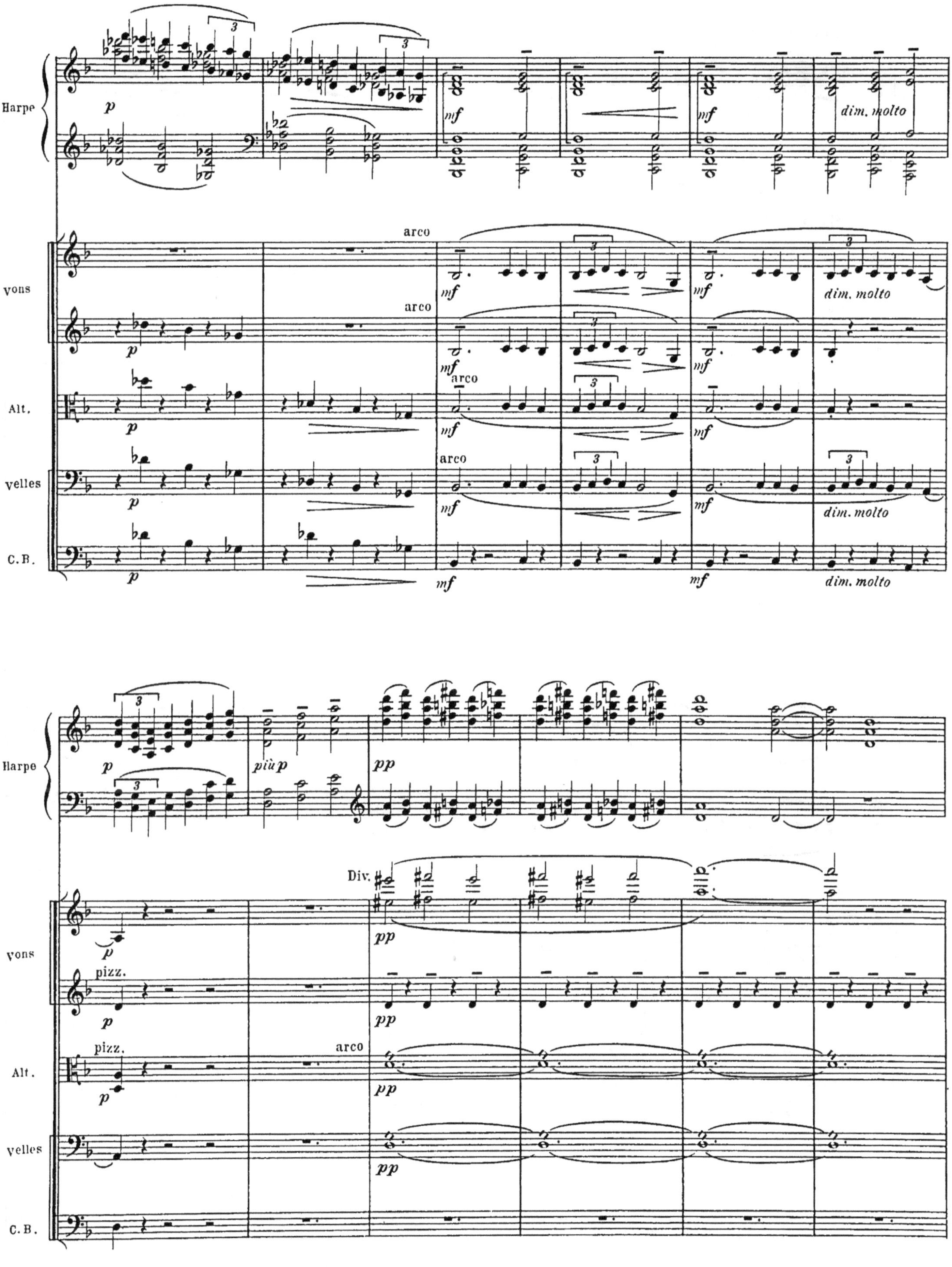
Harpe
vons
Alt.
velles
C.B.
p
mf
dim. molto
arco
più p
pp
Div.
pizz.

Sans lenteur
Harpe
p très expressif
Sans lenteur
vons
arco
pp
Alt.
velles
C.B.
Harpe
p
più p
pp
Solo
vons
p très expressif
più p
pp
p
più p
pp
Solo
Alt.
p très expressif
più p
pp
velles
C.B.

1
En animant peu à peu
Harpe
p
cre - - scen - - do
En animant peu à peu
pizz
pp
vons
Alt.
velles
C.B.
pizz.
Harpe
p
dim.
p
vons
Div.
arco
pp
dim.
p
arco
pp
Alt.
dim.
p
velles
C.B.

Harpe
pp cre - - scen - - do
f
Div.
arco
mp cre - - scen - - do
Unis.
Vons
Unis.
mp cre - - scen - - do
Alt.
mp cre - - scen - - do
arco
Velles
p cre - - scen - - do
C. B.
Harpe
f
dim.
p
p cresc. molto
Vons
f
dim.
p
Alt
f
dim.
p
Velles
f
dim.
p
C. B.

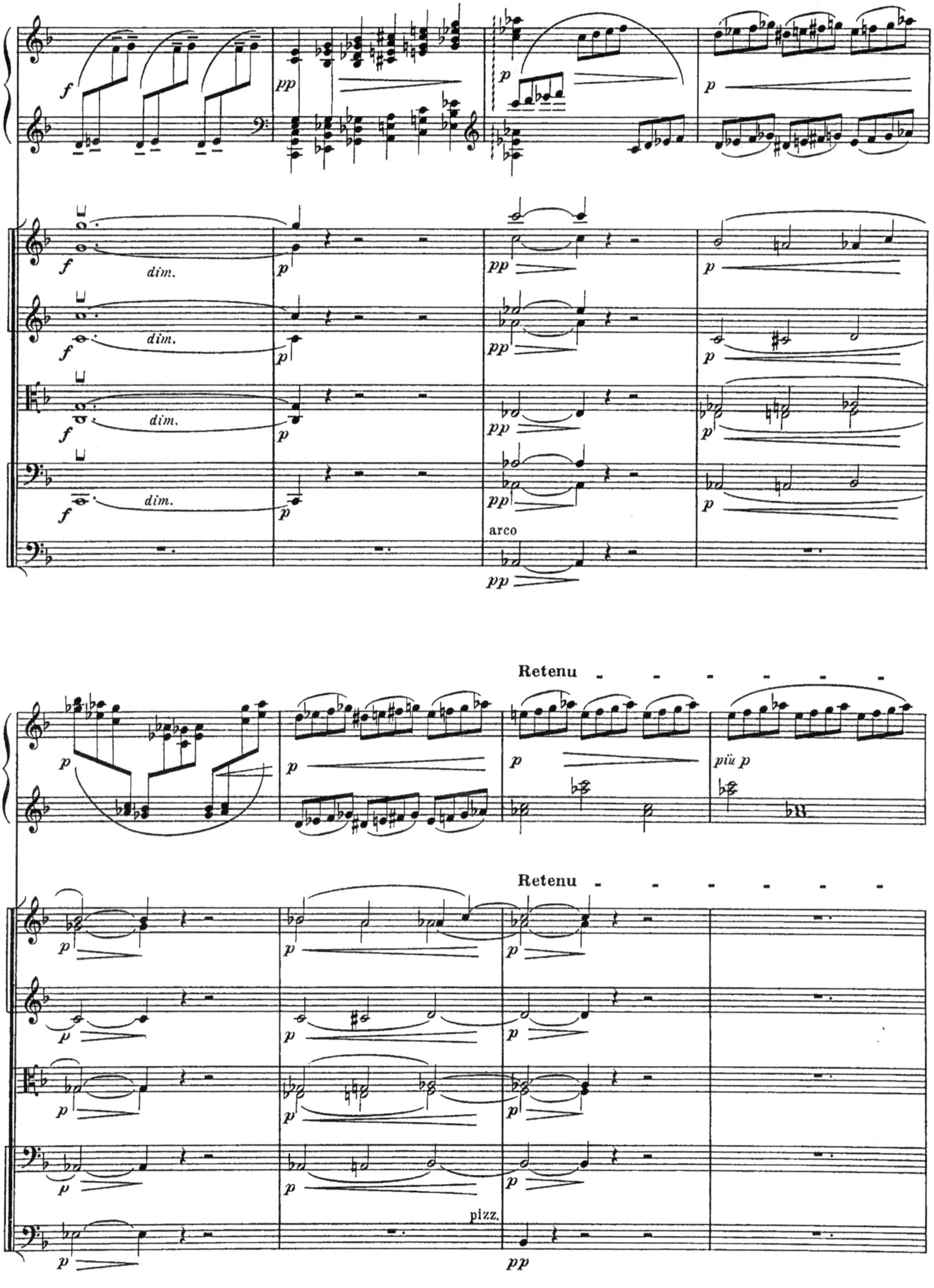
Harpe
vons
Alt.
velles
C. B.
dim.
arco
Retenu
pizz.
più p

2
1º Tempo
Harpe
3
pp
1º Tempo
vons
pp doux et expressif
Alt.
velles
C.B.
pizz.
arco
doux et expressif
p
mettez les sourdines
Div.
più p

Harpe
pp
Vons
pizz
pp
mettez les sourdines
Alt.
pizz
pp
mettez les sourdines
velles
pizz.
pp
C. B.
arco
ppp
Harpe
più pp
Retenu
sempre pp
Vons
Retenu
Alt.
velles
C. B.
Enchaînez

II. Danse profane

Animez
Harpe
p poco a poco cresc.
più cresc.
Animez
ôtez les sourdines
Vons
ôtez les sourdines
ôtez les sourdines
Alt.
pizz.
più cresc.
pizz.
velles
p poco a poco cresc.
più cresc.
C.B.
pp
più cresc.
Harpe
f
dim.
pizz.
Vons
f
dim.
pizz.
f
dim.
Alt.
velles
C.B.
f
dim.

Rit.
1º Tempo
Harpe
p
Rit.
1º Tempo
arco
pp
Vons
p
Alt
velles
C B
Harpe
p
Vons
Div.
p
Alt.
velles
C.B.

Harpe
vons
Alt.
velles
C. B.
p cre - scen - do
pizz.
p cre - scen - do
Harpe
vons
Alt.
velles
C. B
3
molto
pizz.
mf cre - scen - do molto
arco
mf
f

14

41731

Animez
Harpe
f
dim.
Animez
vons
f
Alt.
velles
C.B.
dim.
Retenu
p
più p
Retenu
pizz.
p
più p

a Tempo
Harpe
pp
a Tempo
arco
pp
vons
arco
pp
Alt.
arco
pp
velles
pp
C.B.
pp
Harpe
pp
vons
pp
pp
Alt.
pp
velles
C.B.

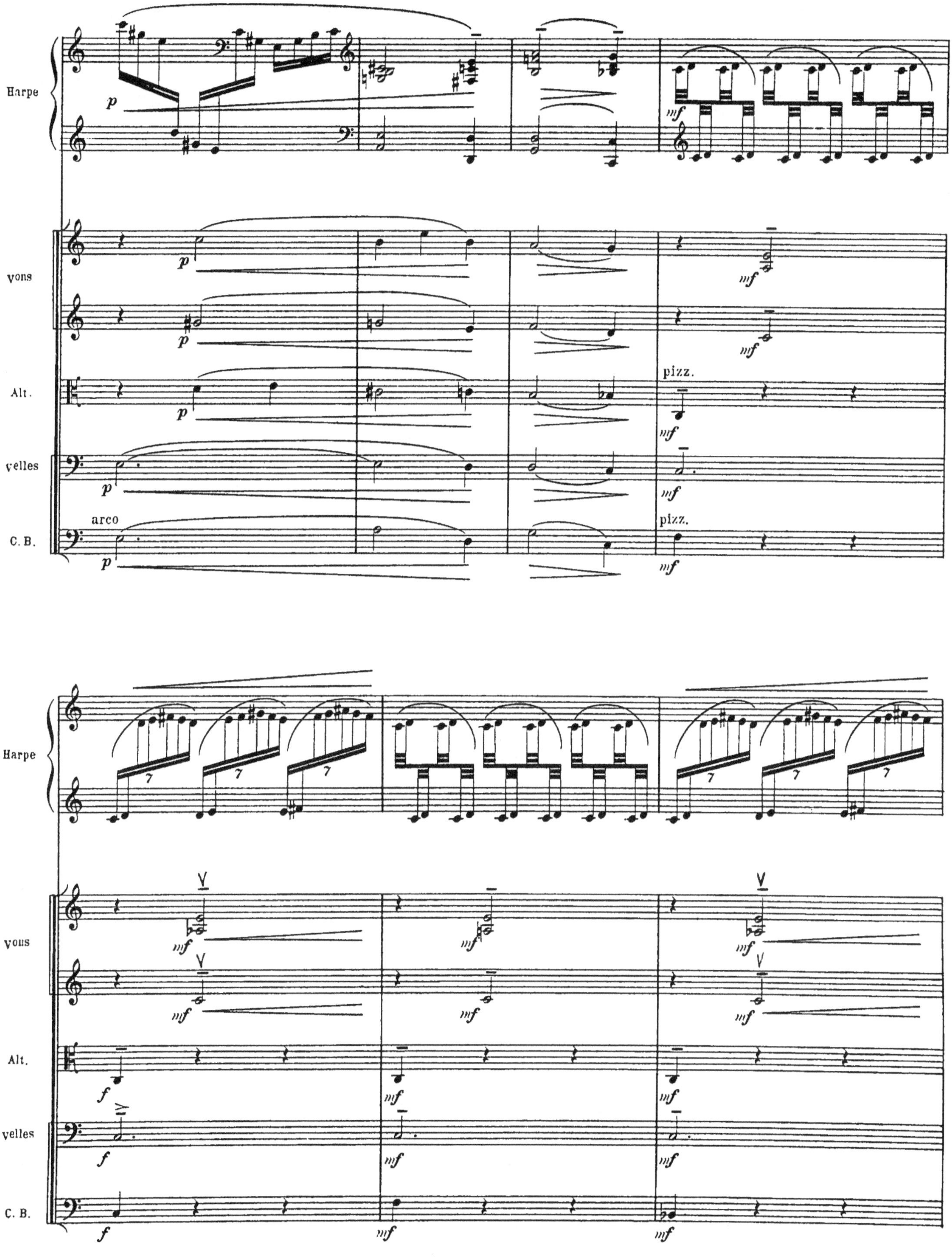
Harpe
vons
Alt.
velles
C. B.
arco
pizz.
p
mf
f

18

41731

Retenu
a Tempo
Harpe
pp
più pp
p
Retenu
a Tempo
vons
Alt.
velles
C. B.
pizz.
Harpe
vons
Alt.
velles
C. B.

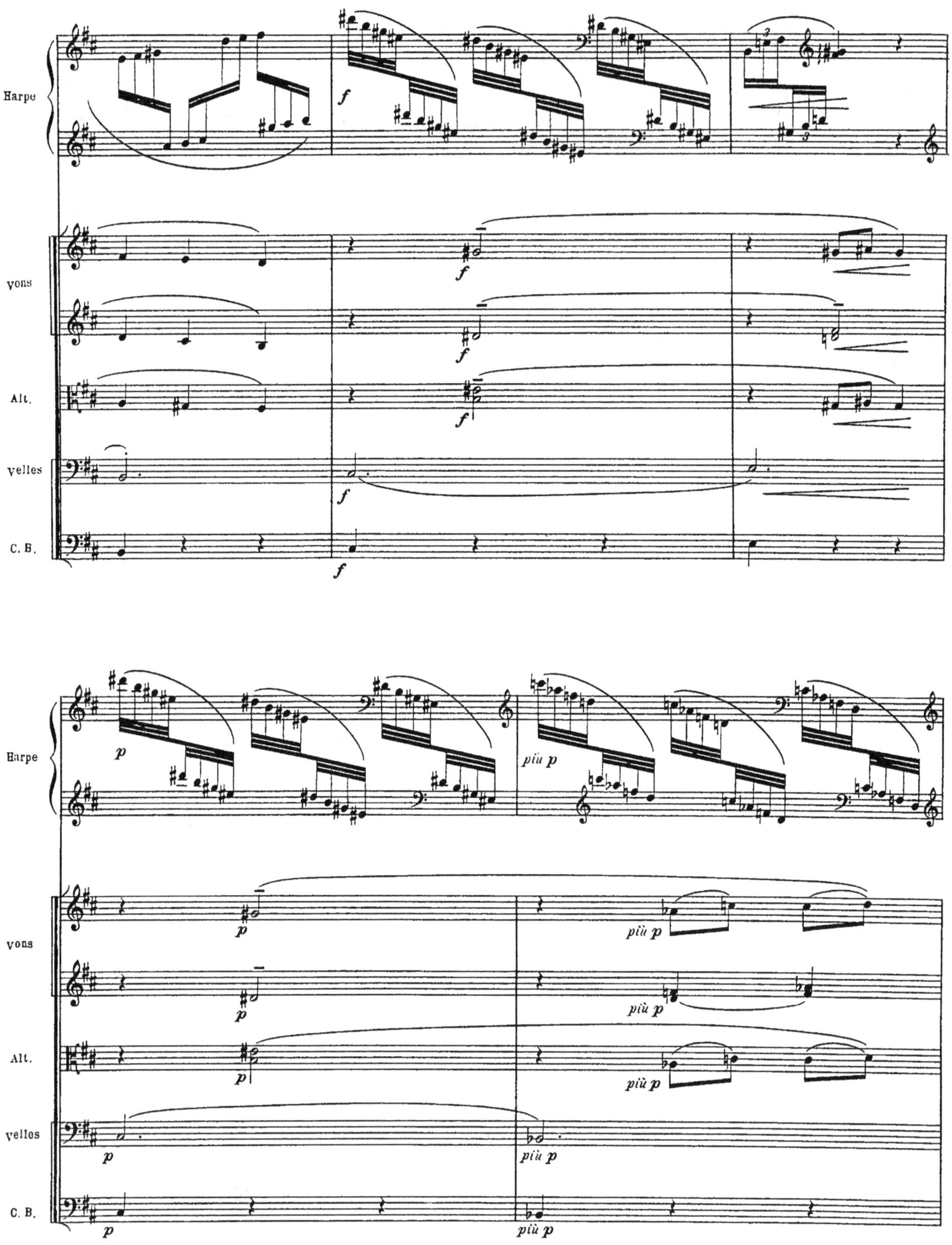
Harpe
vons
Alt.
velles
C. B.
f
p
più p

Très retenu

Harpe

Très retenu

vons

Alt.

velles

C.B.

Le double moins vite (Tempo rubato)

Harpe

piu p

mp doux et expressif

Le double moins vite (Tempo rubato)

mettez les sourdines

vons

piu p

Div.

piu p

mettez les sourdines

Alt.

piu p

mettez les sourdines

velles

piu p

pp

mettez les sourdines

arco

C.B.

piu p

pp

22

41731

5
Harpe
f
Unis.
f très expressif
Vons
f
Alt.
f
velles
f très expressif
C. B.
f
Rit.
Plus lent et retenu
Harpe
dim.
p
più p
pp
Rit.
Plus lent et retenu
ôtez les sourdines
Vons
dim.
ôtez les sourdines
dim.
ôtez les sourdines
Alt.
dim.
p
ôtez les sourdines
velles
dim.
p
C. B.
dim.
p

a Tempo (Animez)
Harpe
f
p
ff
a Tempo (Animez)
pizz.
sf
Vons
Alt.
Velles
C. B.
dim
molto
Retenu
p

1° Tempo (Un peu plus mouvementé)
Harpe
pp
p
1° Tempo (Un peu plus mouvementé)
arco
pp
Vons
Alt.
Velles
pizz.
C. B.

26

41731

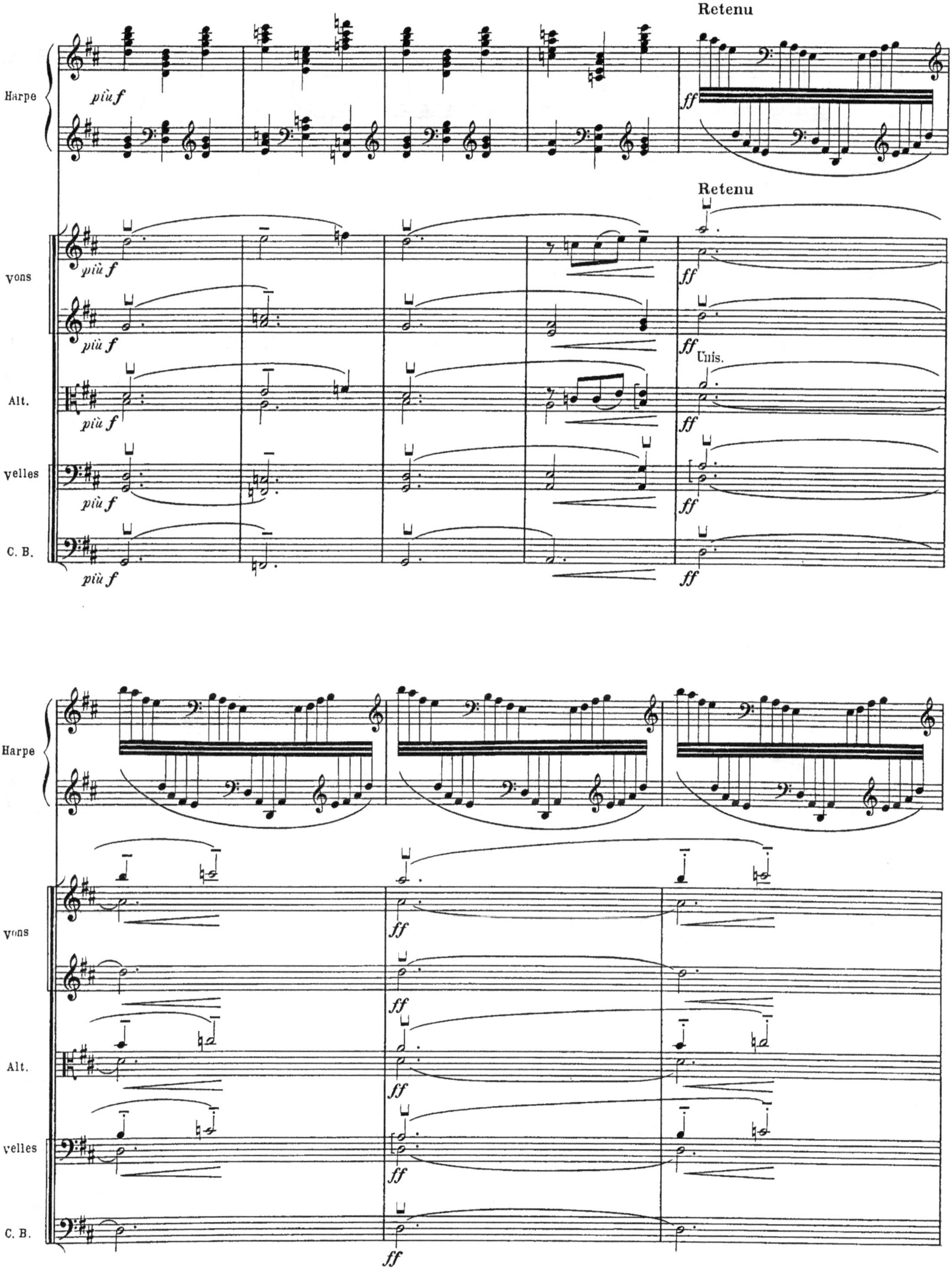
Retenu
Harpe
più f
ff
Retenu
Vons
più f
ff
Unis.
Alt.
velles
C. B.

Ch. Douin gr._ Poinçons A. Durand & Fils.

FIN

www.ingramcontent.com/pod-product-compliance
Lightning Source LLC
Chambersburg PA
CBHW081235020426
42331CB00012B/3178